William Bolcom

Aubade
for the Continuation of Life

for Oboe or B♭ Soprano Saxophone and Piano

NOTE

Aubade, written for Heinz Holliger and Dennis Russell Davies, was inspired by a reading of Jonathan Schell's *The Fate of the Earth*, with its alarming projection of nuclear holocaust. It is a quiet, elegaic piece, subtitled "For the Continuation of Life." Holliger and Davies premiered the work in Helsinki in September 1982.

Harry Sargous, professor of oboe at the University of Michigan, and I have since recorded Aubade on Crystal CD326. The work has seen a number of performances by other oboists as well as performers on the

for Heinz Holliger & Dennis Russell Davies

AUBADE

for the Continuation of Life

for Oboe or B♭ Soprano Saxophone and Piano

WILLIAM BOLCOM
(1982)

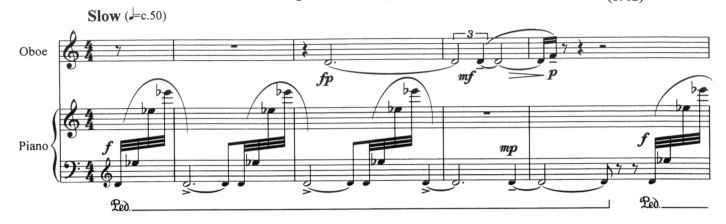

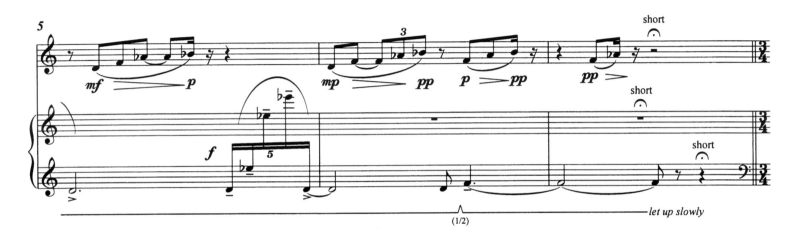

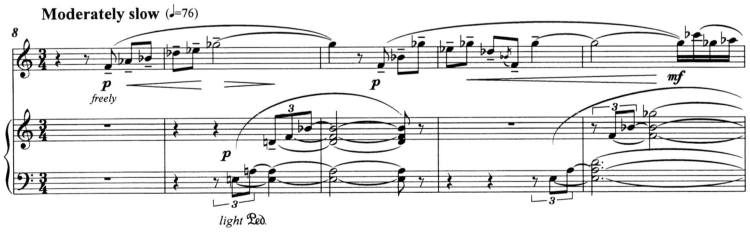

**B♭ SOPRANO
SAXOPHONE**

for Heinz Holliger & Dennis Russell Davies

AUBADE
for the Continuation of Life
for Soprano Saxophone and Piano

WILLIAM BOLCOM
1982

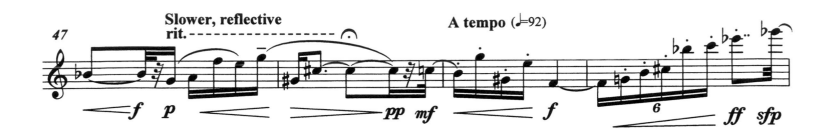

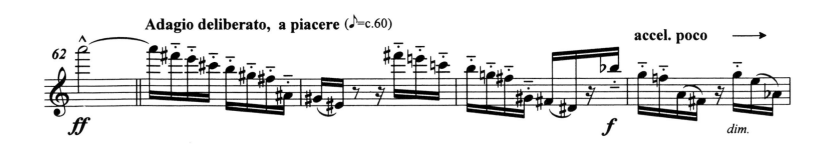

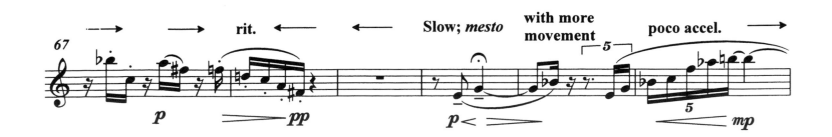

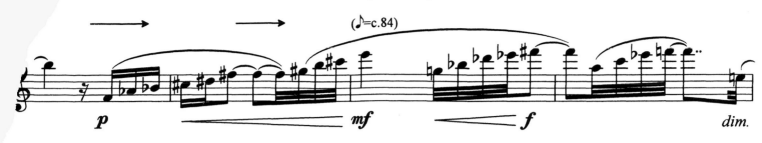

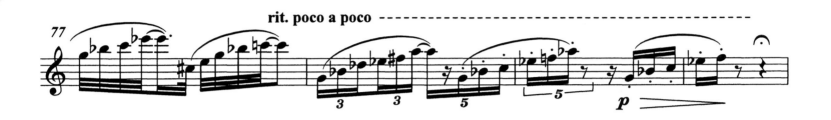

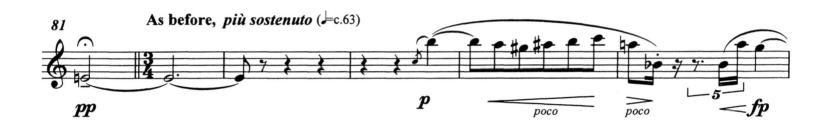

for Heinz Holliger & Dennis Russell Davies

AUBADE
for the Continuation of Life
for Oboe and Piano

WILLIAM BOLCOM
1982

OBOE

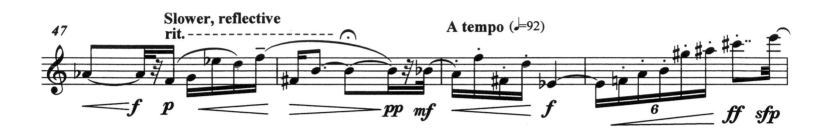

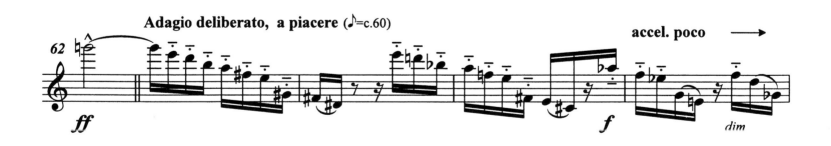

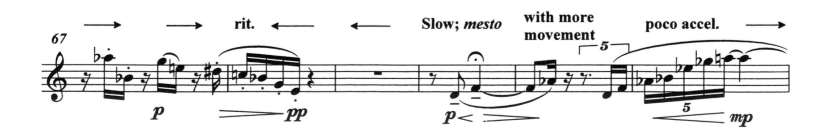

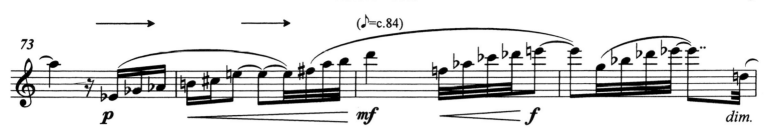

73

rit. poco a poco -

77

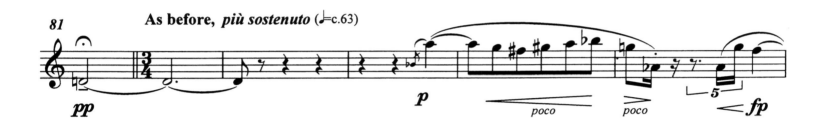

As before, *più sostenuto* (♩=c.63)

81

87

94

100

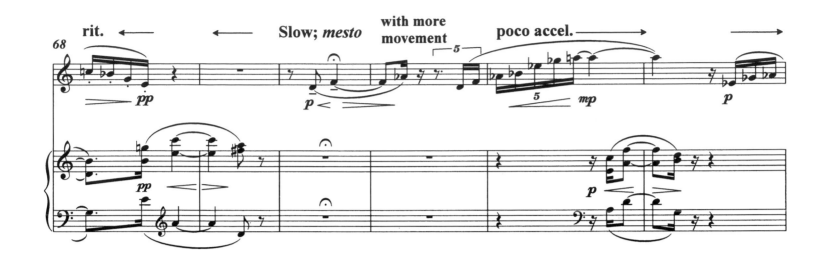

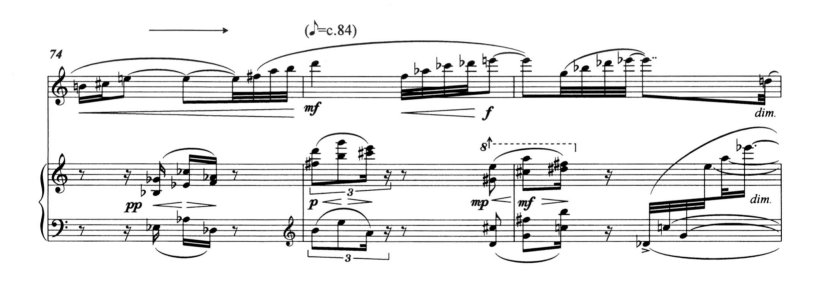